MAKING LIFE MORE DELICIOUS

The Secret Recipe for a
Flavor-Filled Work Culture

MAKING LIFE MORE DELICIOUS

The Secret Recipe for a Flavor-Filled Work Culture

RÉMON M. KARIAN

ethos
collective

Published by Ethos CollectiveTM
PO Box 43, Powell, OH 43065
EthosCollective.vip

LCCN:2023902497
Paperback ISBN: 978-1-63680-119-3
Hardback ISBN:978-1-63680-120-9
e-book ISBN:978-1-63680-121-6

Available in paperback, hardcover, and e-book

DEDICATION

This book is dedicated to my wife, Genevieve, my daughter, Karina, my family, and my team.

TABLE OF CONTENTS

What's Inside…

PART III

INTRODUCTION

Jerry and Margaret[1] frequently eat at Fiorella's. Every hostess knows their favorite table, and most waitstaff can fill their drinks before ordering. Even the chefs recognize their special requests. The atmosphere brightens when their familiar faces enter the room.

For a short season, Margaret dined alone. As you might imagine, it worried me, so I stopped and asked about her husband.

"He's out of town visiting his parents."

"I'm glad to see you're still coming on your own.".

Her smile warmed my heart. "No place feels quite so comfortable as Fiorella's."

I appreciated her kind words; however, I knew this long-time customer would have felt the same even if I'd taken the night off. My staff works full-time to make Fiorella's a dining experience patrons remember for months. The ambiance made Margaret feel at home, from the inviting décor and warm staff to the delicious food and friendly vibe, which didn't happen by accident. The entire staff dedicated themselves to creating a welcoming environment. The success at Fiorella's took a lot of failures and fretting. But through it all, we learned a great deal about how to do the restaurant thing right.

OUR MISSION

We are passionate about making you smile,
one meal at a time, every time.

Unfortunately, too many establishments live up to the industry's reputation for treating employees poorly. Though some find Gordon Ramsay's signature shouting entertaining, those in the food service industry know the reality is anything but inspiring. In fact, too many chefs and restaurateurs create a demeaning culture that sometimes becomes downright abusive.

The energy requirements and high-intensity nature of food service chew people up and spit them out. Hostesses and waitstaff endure abuse from customers, and bussers find messes you would never imagine. Even chefs and cooks feel the stress as special orders and dietary restrictions force them to take extra time to plate meals. Few realize the demands put on a crew that depends on the generosity of the clientele to bring them a living wage. So, when management adds to that burden with unrealistic expectations or by treating employees as replaceable, it takes a desperate or extremely tough-skinned individual to stick it out.

I believe we can do better.

A long time ago, I decided I didn't want to be the guy screaming at everyone as if they were the problem. I want to inspire a team by treating them right. So Fiorella's mission to bestow a smile on each of our patrons extends to our team. At least a dozen employees have been with Fiorella's for over ten years—some have been part of our family for fifteen or twenty years. They will all tell you—we may not be perfect, but we definitely have something special.

MY TIME IN THE TRENCHES

Like many in the business, I worked my way up from busing tables and mopping floors at my dad's pizzeria to the dishwasher and then line cook in a diner. I've seen chefs get up in people's faces spitting mad, and more than one chef has laughed at me when I burned a dish or dropped a plate. Some days, I couldn't even keep up with all the orders.

Getting my face burned with a sauté pan may have been my worst experience. The chef and I stood side-by-side on a hot cooking line during a busy shift. He pulled a sauté pan out of the oven and needed to put it under the broiler on the other side of me. Rather than walk around me, he muscled his arm over and hit me in the face with the sizzling pan. Then he called me a wimp for complaining about the pain.

Maybe all that yelling makes for good TV, but it doesn't make for good business. Not in my book.

I've worked every position possible in a restaurant and experienced every possible emotion a restaurant worker can feel.

All that experience makes me passionate about creating a different kind of workplace. My wife and I want Fiorella's to be a place where team members feel like family and enjoy a quality of life that supports their individual goals and dreams.

In the early days, I ran the business with just a couple of employees I couldn't afford to lose and couldn't afford to pay. As we grew, I had to learn how to hire well, and then we had to help people develop a new mindset that shattered their expectations of a restaurant always being a toxic workplace.

Eventually, our culture began to crystallize, and we came together as a team to formalize it in what we now call our Five Core Values.

Everything we do is based on: *Making life more delicious*. It's our why, our purpose, and our guiding light. It's the heartbeat of everything Fiorella's stands for.

In this book, we want to share Fiorella's way with you. You're about to become part of our story, and your story will become part of our story. Let's make life more delicious together.

PART I

1

THE FIRST DAYS OF FIORELLA'S

It all began when my Armenian French dad and Armenian Lebanese mother opened a little restaurant. In the mid-1980s, no one had heard of Armenian food, so this Armenian-French-Lebanese family started an Italian pizzeria. Because, after all, who doesn't like pizza?

I grew up in that pizza shop. Cafe Fiorella was your typical, fast-casual, counter-service pizza place. In this family-run business, every person did everything. I took orders, made the food, washed dishes, worked the counter, and put the money in an old-school cash register. There was no back of the house or front of the house; it was all one. In addition to pizza, we offered salads, sandwiches, and a couple of simple pasta dishes like pasta primavera with garlic and oil or fettuccine alfredo with broccoli—all cooked on an electric hot plate. I learned to make it all.

Eventually, I graduated as a pizza maker, operating an iconic wood-burning brick oven. Finessing that oven was more of an art than a science, and it cooked the pizza *fast*.

I discovered early that I loved experimenting with new dishes. I tested spices and explored creative combinations. My favorite meals were off-menu— funky pizzas and calzones full of pesto, mushrooms, prosciutto, and onions. When you eat pizza every day, you start trying new things to change it up.

I learned everything from my dad, both good and bad. Dad demonstrated eternal patience as I started getting my own ideas about how I would run things differently. He listened and nodded, and once in a while, he tried one of my changes. He had his own ideas and habits, but he kept an open mind. And he taught me that those two things, patience, and an open mind are keys to growth in a business like this.

Most importantly, Dad invested in people. He had natural charisma, but his success came from the community he formed around his personality. Employees felt welcomed and valued, creating a team loyal to him. Customers considered him a friend. After I expanded and brought the original store back into the family, many of Dad's former guests and staff visited, telling me stories of how he had made them feel welcome and important. He left big shoes to fill.

My father also showed me how hard this job can be. Dad *was* Café Fiorella's. If it was open, he was there. We closed on Sundays so he could have a day off. Everything centered on him. Later, I told him I had worked a double at another restaurant. He said, "What's a double?" When I explained, he smirked and said, "That's just called going to work."

When I started dreaming about my own place, I wanted to improve on the good and learn from the bad. I continually look for ways to make things work better and more smoothly. After watching my dad, I wanted to create a business that could run without me. I also wanted to bring Fiorella's into more neighborhoods.

The business school at Bentley University allowed me to build on everything Dad had taught, but I grew impatient with theories and wanted to put them into practice. At twenty-three, I wrote a business plan and shopped it to five banks.

They all turned me down. Banks didn't like lending to restaurants because they had such a high failure rate. Especially, a twenty-three-year-old bright-eyed kid…

The roadblock only made me more focused and determined to succeed. Dad had taught me that failure was not an option. Luckily, my parents believed in me and my vision. They co-signed a loan so I could get the capital I needed to start my own business. And they put up the equity in their home for collateral. I found a location I could afford off the beaten path. The price also meant the space needed a lot of love. I poured everything I had into getting it open. I spent hours on my hands and knees, making the tile floors sparkle.

Failure was not an option.

THE FIORELLA'S FEEL

In June of 2000, I opened my first location. My brother, Dad, and I all worked the line for Fiorella's Newton grand opening. It was surreal, joyful, and terrifying all at once.

During those first years, I wore every hat—usually at the same time. I greeted guests and escorted them to their table right before I talked up the specials and took their orders. Then I cooked their meals, bussed the tables, and opened the door for them on the way out. It looked like some comedy sketch. Every time the guests turned around; the same guy appeared in a different uniform.

It's a wonder anyone came back. The service was inefficient, I looked harried and tired most of the time, and the whole thing was held together by sheer force of will more than any grander vision.

I later learned that some guests returned out of pity but also seemed to love the food and the warm, genuine hospitality. Often too tired to go home, I slept in the restaurant. I had worked at other restaurants and internalized a lot of the negative food service culture during my college days. Plus, I was the life of the party in high school and college. The first person who had to learn Fiorella's Way was me.

As I grew and thought about what I wanted my restaurant to look like, I knew I wanted people to have fun. I had been a social planner in college and worked as a promoter for a while. Fun wasn't about being the loudest person or acting like a clown but about helping others feel comfortable and welcome.

Second, I wanted to capture the feel of my uncle's dinner table on a Sunday afternoon. My extended family gathered around my uncle's giant dining table every Sunday for a huge, loud family meal. As cousins and aunts grew and started their own families, we added a kid's table in the living room.

Everything in my family centered around food. On any occasion, any emotion could be fed. Family get-togethers always offered an abundance of food and laughter—as well as occasional tears. When we weren't eating, we were shouting over each other. Come to think of it; we shouted even when we were eating. In my mind, love and affection always come in the context of "organized chaos."

That's the feeling I wanted for Fiorella's—comfortable and welcoming, a family atmosphere that gets loud sometimes. I began to see Fiorella's as a place where the staff laughed with the customers, I started to envision a restaurant that made everyone feel at home.

2

A FORMULA FOR GROWTH

Good food and warm hospitality created the growth we needed, allowing me to hire more team members. Several still work with us, a testament to their loyalty as well as Fiorella's culture.

Bringing on additional employees introduced a new learning curve, and much of my education came through mistakes. Not all of my staff choices made for a good fit, and I neglected properly training them. At times, I got caught up in my own problems and took them out on my team. The growth transition became a journey. But I quickly realized I needed to model the kind of person I wanted my team to be.

Eventually, I learned working in the business wasn't enough. I needed to work *on* it. Slowly, I developed the principles and processes that made it possible to expand to multiple locations.

Fiorella's Express in Brighton opened mostly by chance. I had never considered an express model before, and the timing could have been better. The venue was too small for a full-service restaurant, hence the express concept. It featured the greatest hits of the original restaurant in a fast-casual setting.

A few years later, the original Fiorella's Cafe space became available. I loved being able to bring that back into the family. Fiorella's Express second location became a reality.

We grew organically, following the lead of our guests. People raved about our signature marinara sauce and asked to take some home, so we started bottling and selling it. When people asked us to serve their corporate events, weddings, and parties, we started the catering service.

Over the years, despite our fair share of ups and downs, we learned how to do hospitality right. Now, other restaurateurs ask me, "What's the secret?" I say, "There's no silver bullet. It's not any one thing; it's all the little things." Once we learned to consider every aspect of the team and guest experience, Fiorella's grew into the kind of restaurant I'd been dreaming of.

As of this writing, we proudly have six Fiorella's locations, including two cucinas in Newtonville, Concord and three Express locations in Belmont, Brighton, Wellesley, and Lexington. We have development plans to add more locations in the months and years ahead. Our goal is to be the favorite Italian restaurant in New England. We are just getting started.

WHAT MAKES US DIFFERENT

Making life more delicious means, we aim to be more than just another Italian restaurant. Serving great food is only part of it. We strive to create a human connection that people will respond to and want to be a part of.

It all begins with our culture, the Fiorella's Way defined by The Five Core Values they help guide us every day.

These Core Values mean work becomes a meaningful part of our team members' lives through a culture of respect and mutual support. We want to continually show appreciation for our team and help them shine. Plus, we build systems that allow for flexibility while providing structure. We created manuals to help guide and train our team. We use technology like slack for communication and online scheduling software, so our teams can access their schedules remotely or swap shifts. We developed our career path of excellence to outline the growth opportunities and career paths for advancement.

Another part of Fiorella's Way included learning to "hire nice." When you get good people on board from the outset, you can train them to do almost anything in the business. To get the best employees, we offer competitive wages and benefits, including generous paid time off and sick pay. Even our part-time team members can earn paid time off. Our team is really excited about our new 401k plan. Additionally, we offer our managers two weeks of vacation each year, and we allow them to earn up to four weeks.

Fiorella's recognizes the value of our employees, so we have developed a career path to help them learn new skills and take on more responsibility. Additionally, our team has created a work family where people believe in and support each other.

Making life more delicious is more than just a motto for our guests. It's also part of our team's experience. Everyone should have fun and share the fun. The proof is in the *budino* (that's Italian for "pudding"), and our goal is to be voted the top employer of choice by our team.

WHY TEAM MEMBERS STAY

The restaurant industry generally has very high turnover, constantly churning employees in and out. Most long-time food service employees have worked in more than a few establishments.

Fiorella's feels fortunate to have an unusually high retention rate—our goal is to keep it at about 90%. We have many team members who have been with us for well over ten years. Though unheard of in our transient industry, people stick with us because they feel respected. We create an atmosphere that allows team members to build a career and find fulfillment and satisfaction in the work.

INSPIRING CREATIVITY, ACCOUNTABILITY, AND HAPPINESS

I believe people want to do the right thing, and every individual has the potential to be better than yesterday. As leaders at Fiorella's, we work to create an environment where our team can grow and develop. Personally, I'm a sponge for knowledge. I love to learn; I'm always looking to innovate, make things better, become more efficient, and optimize while giving my team the tools they need to succeed. As a team, we realize that believing in one another allows people to spread their wings and confidently try new things.

We're an entrepreneurial company, and we want our employees to have an ownership mentality. Our team doesn't have the typical employee attitude—just doing the minimum work to keep your manager happy--they have embraced the idea of making life more delicious for their colleagues and our guests.

We learn by doing. The Five Core Values exist to empower our team to make decisions on their own. They allow me to provide guidance and a framework to help Fiorella's staff make decisions like I would make when I'm not present.

Several members of the Fiorella family have grown with our company. One of our Area Managers began as a cashier. We set her on the career path and helped her develop into a shift manager and general manager. She then became our office manager, and now she's an area manager running operations for several stores. She accomplished all that in only eight years!

Another team member started as a dishwasher and eventually became a busboy, then a server—a position he held for many years. During his eighteen years with us, he was able to save enough to buy a house to raise his family. His is one of many proud team member stories from our career path to excellence.

Supporting our team and setting them up for success has been a key element in the development and family-like atmosphere

FUN FACT: FIORELLA IS A FEMALE NAME OF ITALIAN ORIGIN THAT MEANS LITTLE FLOWER[2].

of our ever-expanding restaurant. Fiorella's Five Core Values undergird this culture of growth and empower our team to be the very best they can be.

PART II

OUR FIVE CORE VALUES:
THE FIORELLA'S WAY

Our core values are the heart of our business. They guide every decision, empower our team and help us grow as a company. These core values didn't come to us overnight. We labored over their creation, giving them, many rounds of revisions over time to get them right.

This cornerstone of our success began as a management team exercise. The entire team spent hours reflecting on who we were and who we wanted to be. While the core values reflect my personality and beliefs, the team collectively created them, making them so much more powerful. These values resonated with everyone.

These are the Five Core Values of Fiorella's Way:

- Hospitality from the Heart
- Integrity in Our Actions
- Take Initiative
- Roll Up Your Sleeves
- Desire to Learn

People are the most important part of our business, and developing our team has become a priority for our leadership team. We push ourselves to nurture and grow future leaders and enthusiastically share the recipe and secret ingredients to our success.

THE THREE-LEGGED STOOL

The Five Core Values work in tandem with the Three-Legged Stool. We use this image to illustrate our thinking about the business, so team members have a framework to make decisions independently. Our team members feel empowered and confident about making decisions that align with the Core Value and the Three-Legged Stool. And each person knows that even if it turns out to be a bad choice, we have their back.

You may be familiar with the image of a three-legged stool. In brief, all three legs must stay firmly planted on the ground. If one of those legs breaks or gets loose, it threatens the stability of the whole thing.

The three legs of Fiorella's stool will not surprise you:

1. Our team
2. Our guests
3. The business

Every decision the members of our team make should take into consideration the effect it will have on each of the three legs. We know we've made the right decision when it's suitable for our team, guests, and the business.

Sometimes our trifecta is more like a tricycle. All three wheels must stay on an even plane; however, the big wheel pulls the other two. In the restaurant industry, the team is the big wheel. We've learned that if we take care of our team, they will take care of the guests, and our business will thrive. If something looks good for business and the guests but will make the team miserable, we either abandon that choice or brainstorm to make it better.

3

CORE VALUE ONE: HOSPITALITY FROM THE HEART

Authentic hospitality comes from the heart and drives everything we do, from our recipes to cooking to interacting with each other and our guests. It is all-encompassing.

Hospitality is not a synonym for *service*. Lots of places provide service. You can get service from a vending machine. Hospitality considers emotions. Service makes food; hospitality creates an experience.

At Fiorella's, hospitality means making guests and team members feel like they're part of a family. Imagine taking a walk on a brisk fall day, and then the sun peeks out from behind some clouds, and you pause for a moment when you feel that warmth on your face. That's how we want our guests to feel when they step through our door. It's a feeling of love, deep satisfaction, and a sense of being present where you are.

27

Hospitality shows up in our actions. Fiorella's customers can see how much we care. And we greet our staff with the same smile and concern we give our guests. Regardless of what our team needs, they know they can ask, and someone will try to help. We hire team members with the goal of growing as a company, not so we can turn them into a cog in some machine.

We want to extend hospitality to our guests, team, vendors, and each other as individuals—anyone we encounter. Hospitality is at the core of making life more delicious because it's about how we make people feel.

HOSPITALITY IS TAKING CARE OF EACH OTHER

Hospitality, in its simplest form, means taking care of each other. At Fiorella's, it begins with taking care of other team members. Our team is incredibly supportive of each other! Though the atmosphere keeps last-minute call-offs to a minimum, when one member of the staff can't come to work for whatever reason, someone else quickly picks up the shift. They know it will be reciprocated. Taking care of one another builds teamwork and helps things run smoothly on the floor.

For instance, when a team member and his family lost everything in an apartment fire, one of our servers organized a fundraiser at the restaurant. She rallied our team and regular guests to be a part of it. We had at least one hundred team members and faithful guests attend and make donations. We raised a substantial amount and collected clothing and toys for the kids. Our team member and his family were deeply moved by the outpouring of support.

On another occasion, a team member was involved in a horrible car accident. While being transported to the hospital, her purse, containing a thousand dollars, came up missing. The team started raising money. Even the guests pitched in so her family would be taken care of while she recovered. I try to model this behavior, but most of my job nowadays is to get out of the way so the team can make their own ideas happen. Seeing them carry out the first core value of Fiorella's makes me extremely proud.

HOSPITALITY IS A FEELING YOU CREATE

We know we've lived up to Fiorella's style of hospitality when we see those smiles. But how do we do that—how can we make everyone smile? First, we have to love what we do—and when it's your job to take care of people, that's not hard to do.

We believe that every experience matters. So each visit to Fiorella's includes consistently delicious food and a welcoming, caring atmosphere. We serve thousands of happy guests a day, but we treat each meal as if it were the most important one.

Think about it: Each person who walks through the door is in the middle of that day's story. They may be tired or in a hurry, excited or anxious. Some are celebrating or going on a first date. This one meal becomes part of that story and that memory. When we do our job right,, feed their souls, and make that memory special. That's an incredible responsibility.

We love having fun and invite our guests to celebrate their birthdays with us. Any guest can sign up for our birthday club and receive a free meal on their special day. It's a simple gesture that guests look forward to every year. There's an old credit card commercial that lists the prices of each step of a company's logistics process: "Printing postcards…so much. Postage…so much. A free meal…so much." Then it ends by showing the effect on the customer: "Making someone feel special on their birthday…*priceless*." That's what we're going for.

Guests have shared many special moments and occasions with us. Our restaurants have been the setting for engagements, weddings, and birthday parties. Our guests have celebrated anniversaries, promotions, graduations, and special religious occasions with us. They've even had Fiorella's catered in their homes. When we connect with others with hospitality from the heart, we send a message that we think of them as family, and they know we mean it.

It's nice to be part of that, and it's nice to feel good about a restaurant. We love when guests come back and tell us about the special memories, they've created at Fiorella's.

HOSPITALITY IS A SENSORY EXPERIENCE

Hospitality includes all five senses. Genevieve, our designer and Creative director, helps us think about the little details of eating at Fiorella's. What do people see, hear, smell, and feel even before they taste our food?

I liked the open kitchen concept well before it was fashionable. With no walls between the front and the back of the house, guests get to see the organized chaos of an efficient kitchen. It's a symphony of sights, sounds, and smells with the Chef as the conductor. Plus, the kitchen staff loves watching the captivated faces or the startled expressions when flames shoot up. Because they can see the hard work that goes into preparing their meal, patrons often stop to thank the chefs and crew personally. This open concept creates a more interactive experience for everyone.

Our dining rooms offer elegant but comfortable designs, spaces where you can come for a fun time with friends or an intimate evening with a loved one. The rustic Italian charm of our locations helps guests relax while also serving as a beautiful setting for celebrations.

Cleanliness, of course, is a big deal in a restaurant. During the pandemic mitigations, we took our cleaning and sanitation procedures to the next level and added some extra features, like UV lighting in our HVAC system and air purifiers, so guests could feel confident we were keeping them (and ourselves) safe.

Many thoughts go into making our hospitality a sensory experience. The lighting gives a warm and soft feel but stays bright enough for guests to see one another down a long table. We don't want the typical elevator music to fill the silence. Instead, we elevate the experience with wonderful Italian dinner music, finding the right vibe and volume, so everyone can have a nice time. Even the number on the thermostat matters. The funny thing about it all is that when all the design elements are working, guests don't notice most of it. They only know how it makes them feel.

HOSPITALITY IS COMMUNITY

Fiorella's now has a place in half-a-dozen communities. We make a point of hiring as many locals as possible and building relationships with the other business owners and community leaders. We have a diverse team of individuals that come together with a common goal. For many, it's their first job. We love the opportunity to watch them grow in our culture. People want to be part of the experience that we provide.

In an effort to give back, we get involved with many fundraisers, working with local schools and charity organizations. We host community events in restaurants and donate a percentage of our proceeds to the organization, which is a nice win-win. Our community hospitality includes donating gift cards or trays of pasta for causes, fundraisers, and helping others.

Involvement in local chambers of commerce and community groups helps us establish relationships with town leaders and other businesses. They help us discover new ways to get involved. We aim to be good neighbors, working together for a common purpose and helping to create vitality for our towns and cities.

Our team members participate in the process. Anyone can recommend an organization they care about. We try to support as many groups as possible and give our team guidance on what it takes to participate and create successful partnerships and community relationships.

4

CORE VALUE TWO: INTEGRITY IN OUR ACTIONS

Everyone knows that integrity is what we do when no one is watching. Our actions create a culture of trust based on honesty, professionalism, and mutual respect. Fiorella's chooses to be a productive, safe, and fun workplace filled with integrity.

A culture of integrity means we respect each other's feelings and do the right thing even when no one is looking. Plus, when people *are* looking, we lead by example. It's the value we place on ourselves. We follow through and follow up. Put simply; integrity means we do what we say we're going to do.

INTEGRITY = THE VALUE WE PLACE ON OURSELVES

Integrity drives Fiorella's to do our best to do the right thing and make sure we are fair and consistent in our words and actions. Integrity builds trust and ultimately represents the value we place on ourselves.

It's one thing to do your job. It's another to treat others respectfully. And it's easy to miss the fact that integrity springs from how we see ourselves. A person of integrity demonstrates respect for themselves, they take more responsibility and treat others generously. We don't use the word love enough in business, but we should…

It's easy to cut corners in business and in the kitchen when no one's looking. When we're having a rough day or feel tired and taken for granted, it's tempting to put off the side work, push your breaks long, or take a little something here or there. It really bothers me to hear of this happening at other restaurants, so at Fiorella's, we try to be extra aware of our actions.

Acting with integrity isn't about not wasting money. It's about respecting yourself, your team, the organization, and the guests. At Fiorella's, we put our trust and confidence in our team. Our managers aren't police officers. They're here to help team members serve the guests better, not to babysit the employee's behavior. In return for the trust, we put in our staff, we insist each team member provide guests with safe, high-quality food and a positive experience.

Sometimes a lack of integrity has serious consequences—food allergies, for instance. As a restaurant, we bear a substantial responsibility to help guests avoid allergens and make sure our kitchen is run properly to avoid cross-contamination. Cutting corners could be deadly in this situation. At the least, it would violate the trust our guests put in us.

Again, integrity can't be created by cracking the whip. It naturally evolves when we have an environment, we can all feel good about. I want my team members to feel proud of the work they do. Hopefully, our hospitality will help every member of our staff recognize their value. We want them to understand they are part of a team and a company that cares about them and the guests we serve because we know the more people value themselves, the higher their level of integrity.

INTEGRITY STARTS AT THE TOP

Integrity doesn't manifest itself just because it's required in an employee handbook. It must be lived out from the top. I never want to let someone down, so I do my best to demonstrate integrity and expect the same from our leaders. Whether it's a training or development opportunity for a team member, paying our vendors on time, or showing up when we say we will, I want people to be able to count on Fiorella's and our staff. We have a responsibility to be our best to everyone we meet—team, guests, vendors, and our community.

Consistency is critical to maintaining integrity with food and leadership. No one likes the idea that someone might be playing favorites. I want our new staff members to know right up front that we work hard to make ethical and fair decisions based on all the information we have at the given time and what we believe is truly best for that three-legged stool.

Being part of a company that you know will do the right thing is unique—especially when it's not easy or may even cost the company a little extra. But if it's the right thing to do, that's the path Fiorella's will take. Hopefully, acting with this kind of integrity will allow our staff to experience the benefits of a workplace where they feel part of a team, can be themselves, and know they will be treated fairly.

FULL TRANSPARENCY

Every business has to make difficult decisions that affect their employees. A company of integrity means the management offers as much transparency as possible. At Fiorella's, this translates into communicating with the team when we make decisions that affect them. The conversation starts with the leadership and continues with the leadership having a discussion with the rest of the team. Our transparency includes an open-door policy, so anyone can come to us when they have ideas or concerns.

Sometimes transparency means owning your mistakes. Humans make mistakes. Integrity calls me to acknowledge those mistakes and to own them.

Hopefully, I learn and grow from them. Admitting mistakes can be difficult, and as someone who has worked on the line, washed dishes, greeted customers, and served diners, I know how easy it is to feel taken for granted. I've been in the thick of it, and many people I worked with side-by-side on the line have seen me grow and been part of my growth.

Part of transparency is respecting each team member and ensuring they understand their importance to me personally as well as to the restaurant. Fiorella's cannot run without someone washing dishes and taking out the trash; those employees are vital and deserve to be treated with dignity and as much respect as an area manager. Integrity is management standing side-by-side with the rest of the team and being human with them. Having full transparency with the team and involving the leadership team in the decision-making process helps to strengthen everyone's confidence.

PERSONAL RESPONSIBILITY

Unfortunately, the food service business isn't known for integrity, so when new employees come out of other restaurant experiences, we give them training so they can see how Fiorella's is different and feel empowered to make decisions when no one is around.

I want team members to know that I understand mistakes happen. When decisions they make don't end well, it's okay as long as they're able to learn from them. Some people are paralyzed by indecision. I'd rather team members take responsibility and make decisions, even if it's wrong than have things left undone or unaddressed. We can learn from our mistakes and move forward. Because we embrace this core value of integrity, we support our staff when they take responsibility for their actions, even when they mess up. We debrief the staff member regarding how they made the decision and what went wrong and talk about how to approach a similar situation next time. No one can control every outcome. If decisions are thought through and made with Fiorella's core values and three legs in mind, things can never truly go wrong, whatever happens.

We appreciate our team members who act with integrity. This quality builds trust among our team and our customers and has become a huge part of Fiorella's and Fiorella's Way.

5

CORE VALUE THREE: TAKE INITIATIVE

Many new team members tremble at the thought of taking the initiative. Some have tried it in previous workplaces and discovered the manager had more of an authoritarian style. Sadly, young employees get reprimanded every day for seeing a problem, taking it upon themselves to find a solution, and carrying their idea through to completion. They've been trained to wait for someone to give them the most obvious instructions.

That's why we call employees team members at Fiorellas. When we work in collaboration with one another, we recognize that the three-legged stool encompasses the experience of everyone who walks through our doors, including the staff. We give team members permission and the opportunity to be a part of working the million little details of day-to-day service together to create a tremendous dining experience for our guests. But this only happens when even the newest member takes initiative and uses the power; we've given them to take action when they see that action is needed.

At Fiorella's, we encourage our team to be proactive. From day one, our managers train new members to look for ways to solve problems and propose improvements when they see weaknesses or inefficiencies. We want every person to have an ownership mentality, to feel like Fiorella's is their place, too.

Think about how you welcome guests into your home or throw a party. How do you want them to feel? We want our guests to enjoy that same warmth and comfort in our restaurants, and it takes every team member to take the initiative to make that happen.

From a team member's perspective, taking initiative means acting. No one can sit back and wait for somebody else to decide what to do. In any successful entrepreneurial company, everyone wears many hats. Nothing is "someone else's problem," and we have to adopt the attitude that when we see things that need to be done that fall outside our scope of work because of time limitations, we have to let the right person know it needs doing. Whether a guest has an issue, or you see something that's not right, it's everyone's responsibility to fix it.

Taking initiative means being involved in whatever it takes to make everything happen—guest satisfaction, taking care of each other, ensuring quality food, helping a teammate, doing the right thing, and each piece of the hospitality experience we've addressed in this book. At Fiorella's, we want every team member to advance and achieve, so taking initiative also includes learning more about areas of the business that appeal to you, following your ambitions, and creating your vision to grow.

NEVER-ENDING IMPROVEMENT

At Fiorella's, we measure success by guest satisfaction, how often they return, and the retention of a happy team. Much of our success can be credited to maintaining a standard of excellence in everything we do while also striving for constant and never-ending improvement.

This happens when our team takes the initiative to create loyalty among our guests by increasing their satisfaction whenever possible. Individual team members have the full support of the company to deliver on that commitment to excellence. The consistency we establish in quality-of-service leaves room for team members to have creative freedom to express themselves and demonstrate their personal commitment to excellence.

For example, our menu is inspired by Italy, primarily a comforting Southern Italian-style red-sauce cuisine. To complement that, we offer daily specials which allow our chefs to explore and get creative. Many of our chefs' original specials have made it onto our permanent menu through this process.

Team member initiative has significant improvements to Fiorella's. These ideas have made us more efficient, reduced waste, and made certain tasks easier to perform. Only the other day, someone made a simple but extremely productive change in the kitchen. I was so happy; it only took me twenty years to figure that out.

Everybody at Fiorella's has the power to be involved and make a difference. And each person who's stayed with us for any length of time has added something to make us who we are today. Our team members allow us to grow. Everyone who takes initiative leaves their mark.

Becoming a Better "You"

Fiorella's has become the land of corporate refugees. Some employees have come from toxic environments. They've had to build a wall around themselves to survive. New team members quickly discover it's safe to take the armor off and breathe easily. Sometimes we have to chip away at that armor. We encourage our staff to be themselves—or a better version of themselves— by creating a space that allows our team members to grow, develop, and love what they do. Bosses who micromanage don't allow employees to be themselves. They never let go and have fun, and they discourage new ideas. When an establishment treats people as if they are replaceable, they will never take initiative. At Fiorella's, we hire new staff because we think they can bring something to Fiorella's by being themselves. We can replace a role, but we cannot replace the individuals that makeup Fiorella's family.

Solving Problems

Taking initiative means solving problems. We encourage our staff to make decisions based on the circumstance, taking into consideration what's right for the team and guests.

For instance, it's our policy not to seat incomplete parties. We're often busy, and this enables us to treat all guests fairly. However, when there isn't a wait, the host might take the initiative to seat them while they wait on the rest of their guests and even bring them water or breadsticks to pass the time.

Our policies and guidelines exist to make life more delicious, not to create rigidity or give someone something to hide behind while being petty. We've learned good things happen when we give the team the freedom to take the initiative to care for our guests.

In one case, a server suggested a digital phone system to replace our old traditional, and inconvenient landlines. This new phone system allowed us to efficiently accommodate our guests' needs. It even allows us to play personal messages and music. That gave us the nudge we needed, and now if we put callers on hold, we can give them information about our hours or our specials.

Encouraging Growth

Taking initiative has been a key to Fiorella's growth. I can't be everywhere simultaneously. I rely on my team and leaders to live our core values and tend to the three-legged stool. When we have a strong culture and build initiative into it, I don't need to worry about things getting done, and I know we can grow because we continually pass our culture to each new hire.

That's why we look for people who believe in our core values and want to work in an environment where there is a shared passion for hospitality and learning. We present our core values to new applicants to make sure it resonates with them. We want people to know who we are and what we stand for. We try not to hire applicants that are just looking for a paycheck, where they can just clock in and clock out., We're probably not the right fit for folks with that kind of work objective, .and that's okay.

We hire nice, meaning we hire based on personality, not experience. We look for positive individuals who can be themselves. We can teach them the rest.

6

CORE VALUE FOUR: ROLL-UP YOUR SLEEVES

When we roll up our sleeves, we're getting ready to get hands-on with something. From washing our hands to digging a ditch, I always have my sleeves rolled up to illustrate my readiness and willingness to help out. At Fiorella's, we use rolling up your sleeves as one of our core values to remind us we believe in hands-on hard work, not just in individual roles but as a team. Teamwork means offering a hand even when the task is "not your job." It also means asking for help. We're all in this together; we succeed or fail together. So, we roll up our sleeves together and get to work!

You won't find clipboard managers walking around and just checking boxes. Even our leaders get involved. When we move into all hands on deck, we mean all hands. I never tell somebody to do something I'm unwilling to do or haven't done myself. When leaders work alongside the team, it builds trust and inspires people to support one another. And the value of this philosophy becomes most evident when things get busy.

Ego should not exist at Fiorella's. Confidence is good, but arrogance will get you into trouble. No one is too good to bus a table or too important to clean up a spill. The same team member that we called in as a barback might make a salad in the kitchen when the chefs get backed up. When our servers see food sitting in the window, they get it out while it's hot, even if it's not on their table. We don't tolerate an out-to-get-someone attitude. Instead, we constantly help one another take care of our guests.

"There's no *I* in team" may read like a cliche, but it's true. Ensuring guests leave happy is everyone's responsibility. Our team members understand that the guests at their colleague's table tonight might be their guests tomorrow. If they experience Fiorella's hospitality and feel like they can trust us, they'll return. When the business does well, it gives the company more resources to invest in the team and make the workplace even better.

Taking Care of Business[3]

When managers participate in Rolling up Your Sleeves, it gives the team confidence in the company's leadership. The newest members learn they will be supported through the battle from day one. Plus, a hands-on leader shows them they will always see follow through. Something as simple as bringing breadsticks to a table when the server gets double or triple-seated or delivering a salad to a table on your way to your next task speaks volumes to an overwhelmed waitstaff.

Rolling Up Your Sleeves furthers our Take Initiative core value, as it should in any business. With this kind of mentality, you'll find chefs helping the line keep up and hostesses filling drinks. Plus, at the end of the day, you'll never see one person left cleaning by himself because if the manager notices the closers haven't had time to scrub the floor or the busser sees the trash needs to be carried out, both jobs get done.

Many businesses leave this core value to the lowest-ranking employees. At Fiorella's, rolling up their sleeves is how our leaders model hospitality, integrity, and initiative on a daily basis. When employees feel supported by their leaders, it inspires them to support one another.

NOBODY LIKES DRAMA

Most companies have that one employee that causes drama, chaos, or both every time they walk through the door. It creates unneeded stress. The entire staff checks the schedule every day to see who will be working with them on the next shift so they can prepare or swap the shift. The Fiorella's Way and our careful hiring practices eliminate that fear. Our team knows that no matter whom they work with, or which manager heads up the shift, they'll be working with positive, supportive people who will roll up their sleeves and dig in to make the life of Fiorella's guests and team more delicious.

7

CORE VALUE FIVE: DESIRE TO LEARN

How would the landscape of small business change if every establishment constantly pushed their team to reach their full potential? Sadly, if we live out this value, we will lose some of our best team members as they move into the careers they were created for. On the other hand, we might find management trainees inside individuals everyone else thought wouldn't even make it as a busboy, and that quiet girl on the prep line may end up being our most warm hostess.

Fiorella's strives to celebrate our team by giving them the desire to learn and emphasizing training and development for the business and individuals. We invest in the potential of our employees and our company by learning together, growing, and raising the bar for excellence. A desire to learn keeps everyone open to new ideas and helps us constantly improve and grow.

Many of our members started as cashiers and trained to become managers; some even moved into area managers. Dishwashers become servers, and prep staff can become chefs. While we know not everyone will be at Fiorella's thirty years from now, we value helping team members move into their dream positions and find ways to train them in the direction they want to grow. There's nothing more rewarding than promoting from within!

FIORELLA'S UNIVERSITY

Most of our team leaders have grown within the company. By working together, we uncovered their strengths and developed them to take on the next role.

We created Fiorella's University to give our team a pathway for continuing education and development. Instruction includes in-house training, external courses, mentoring, and job shadowing. We want them to explore and achieve by learning and mastering new skills.

Course topics include leadership, human resources, finance, emotional intelligence, and coaching. Every module focuses on innovation and fostering new ideas and methods. We continually watch for ways to improve these offerings.

Good candidates for Fiorella's University have certain qualities, including:

- Coachability
- Confidence
- Humility

- Approachability
- A servant-leader mentality
- Consistency
- Resiliency
- Compassion/patience
- Optimism
- Leadership presence

Because we hire nice and train the rest, most members of our team have the qualifications necessary. We encourage every team member who would like to move up in our company to talk to us. As we emphasize this core value of the desire to learn, we look for ways to develop the skills and capacities of the team members who step up and enroll in Fiorella's University. Skills take time to develop, and Fiorella's University exists to enable our team members to grow as leaders.

Each leader on Fiorella's team has been charged with finding ways to develop the team members they work with. We expect them to encourage the team, reinforce positive behavior, and acknowledge and appreciate achievements. Our leaders strengthen team members and instill in them this desire to learn. That's how we grow and create an organization of future leaders who fit our culture and philosophy.

GREAT COACHING IS KEY

My dad once told me that we never stop learning. Life is not a destination; it's a journey. We learn and get better by asking questions, role-playing, and learning from each other. Fiorella's is different from many organizations because we invest in our team members and help them develop leadership skills. We prioritize the younger leaders who want to learn and grow.

Leaders at Fiorella's do more than just manage their team or location. They also coach, helping everyone on their team become their best selves.

Here's a little secret: When you help others grow by training them and empowering them in your business, you not only help your business thrive, but you also cultivate that ownership mentality. When people feel like there's no barrier between them and leadership, they feel more connected to their work and want to learn as much as possible about the job.

The desire to learn is a core value because it helps us be better than we were yesterday. Anyone with that desire will be successful and can grow. Fiorella's looks for team members who have that desire to learn and are willing to keep an open mind. We are happy to help them on that journey.

We want Fiorella's to be more than a workplace. We want it to be a place where our members feel welcome and valued, a place that allows them to take action and be hands-on, and most of all, to be a place for continuing education and development—a place to learn, improve, and grow and make their lives a little more delicious each day.

PART III

EMBRACING FIORELLA'S WAY

8

BRING FIORELLA'S WAY TO YOUR BUSINESS

We are proud of the culture we've developed within our team and the way we share it with our guests and our larger community. We believe serving guests a meal is our sacred obligation. It's intimate and special; when we do it right, we become part of their lives.

Fiorella's Way doesn't have to be limited to our team or even restaurants. Any business that wants to raise the bar in its work environment and provide an above-average customer experience can implement our core values. With a bit of tweaking to fit your specific organization and training so that your employees get on board, this model has the potential to create a more positive work atmosphere and even increase the success of your business.

Our team would love to have you visit one of our locations in Massachusetts and see us in action. You'll see how hospitality, integrity, initiative, and team members who roll up their sleeves and have the desire to learn can create an ambiance that's noticeable the moment you walk through the door.

Imagine how the world would change if every small business could create an environment that makes life more delicious.

BEING PART OF FIORELLA'S TEAM

While I hope this book can help others create a more positive workplace, I wrote it to help new members of Fiorella's team understand our Five Core Values and the three-legged stool model.

Welcome to Fiorella's family. Fiorella's Way is all about working hard together, supporting one another through mistakes and accidents, and celebrating success together. We enjoy a special culture of hospitality and integrity that goes all the way back to an immigrant family's pizza parlor.

Maybe you felt stifled in a previous environment and relegated to a role that didn't give you room to develop. That's probably why you're here with us now.

As you begin walking this journey with us, I want you to know that we already see your potential. We value the talents you bring to our team. I ask you the things I ask of myself and the rest of the team. How will you uphold the Five Core Values of Fiorella's? How will you help us be better versions of ourselves? How will you find ways to grow during your time with us? How will you make our lives more delicious?

You're now part of Fiorella's family. As we grow, you will become one of our culture makers, passing down our core values to the team members after you. One year, two years, five years from now, I think we're going to be a different company because of something you bring to the table.

Food is our Foundation. People are our Passion.
Let's make life more delicious together.
—*Rémon*

ABOUT THE AUTHOR

Rémon has been cooking and entertaining guests since the age of 13, when he worked afternoons and weekends in his father's popular brick-oven pizzeria, the original Cafe Fiorella, in Belmont. It was there that Rémon discovered his love for hospitality and innate flair for business. Those formative experiences working alongside his father would become the building blocks for Fiorella's in Newton, where he recreated and expanded on many of his father's recipes. He also credits his Armenian heritage for the family values, sense of tradition, and passion for flavor that are the hallmarks of Fiorella's today.

After pursuing a business degree at Bentley University, Rémon started Fiorella's at 23 with a little more than an entrepreneurial appetite and a vision for delicious rustic food and great service that would win hearts and palates. Fourteen years later, Fiorella's has become one of Newton's culinary gems, and with the addition of Fiorella's Express in Brighton and Belmon (opened in 2011 in the same location as his father's original cafe), Rémon's vision continues to flourish and grow. Fueled by an adventurous spirit, Rémon is in constant pursuit of new ideas, exploring new flavors while respecting tradition. With his innovative vision, tireless dedication, and the help of a talented team, Fiorella's will continue to delight customers for years to come.

MAKE FIORELLA'S SAUCES A STAPLE IN YOUR PANTRY.

Our *beloved* family recipe delivered right to *your* doorstep.

FiorellasMarket.com

FIORELLA'S

CURIOUS?

JOIN OUR TEAM

*Fiorella's is seeking dedicated, energetic
people to join our team.*

If you are passionate about serving quality
food and being part of an outstanding guest
experience, we'd love to meet you!

TO APPLY VISIT
Fiorellas.com/careers

INSPIRATION
SINCE
1986
FROM ITALY

MAKE LIFE *more* DELICIOUS

HOSPITALITY
SINCE
1986
FROM THE HEART

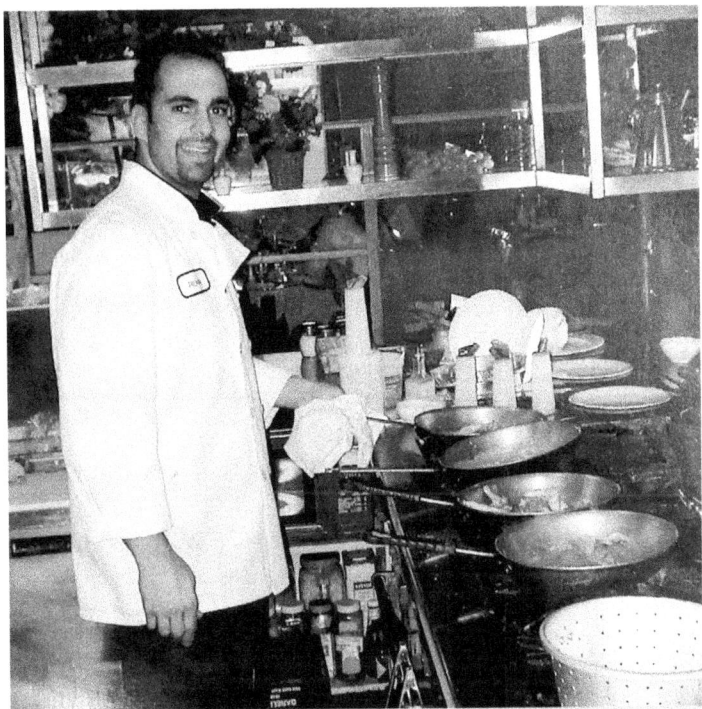

FIORELLA'S

Visit us at Fiorellas.com

INSPIRATION FROM ITALY · SINCE 1986

MAKE LIFE *more* DELICIOUS

HOSPITALITY FROM THE HEART · SINCE 1986

FIORELLA'S

CONNECT WITH US

follow us on all of your favorite social media platforms

🅕 📷 in

THIS BOOK IS PROTECTED INTELLECTUAL PROPERTY

EASY IP™

The author of this book values Intellectual Property. The book you just read is protected by Easy IP™, a proprietary process, which integrates blockchain technology giving Intellectual Property "Global Protection." By creating a "Time-Stamped" smart contract that can never be tampered with or changed, we establish "First Use" that tracks back to the author.

Easy IP™ functions much like a Pre-Patent™ since it provides an immutable "First Use" of the Intellectual Property. This is achieved through our proprietary process of leveraging blockchain technology and smart contracts. As a result, proving "First Use" is simple through a global and verifiable smart contract. By protecting intellectual property with blockchain technology and smart contracts, we establish a "First to File" event.

Powered By Easy IP™

LEARN MORE AT EASYIP.TODAY